Possessing the Land through Home Ownership

A Buyers Guide

POSSESSING
THE LAND THROUGH
HOMEOWNERSHI
(A BUYERS GUIDE)

BY PATRICIA ANN GOLDEN

TABLE OF CONTENTS

DEDICATION

This book is dedicated first of all to my Lord and Savior Jesus Christ. Who from the beginning gave me a purpose and a love to help His people through this process of Home/Land ownership.Then to all the clients that entrusted me to help them with one of the biggest and most expensive decisions/investments in their life.I only hope that the services that I provided made your experience a lot easier. Also, I would like to give special recognition to all of the leaders in my life that guided me and held me accountable for the way I handled God's people. I would like to recognize all those people that referred me to others, and loan officers that God placed around me who believed and trusted in me as a Real Estate Agent. I even thank God for those that chose not to use me as a Real Estate Agent, because it showed me how valuable I was to those that willingly listened to the guidance and accomplished the American Dream of Homeownership.

FOREWORD BY
DOCTOR DURANE HEPBURN
PASTOR OF JUMP (JOYOUSLY
(UNVEILING THE MASTERS PLAN)
MINISTRY

I have been Pastoring for over 27 years and received an Honorary Doctorate degree for my work with the community. I understand intimately the obstacles that members face in accomplishing their dreams. Oftentimes people have a mindset that they cannot have more and they settle for less. Over the years, i have encouraged my members to shift their thinking and believe that they can have anything they want with the right
resources, I have known the writer of this book, Patricia Golden, for many years to be a person that also helps people see beyond only being able to rent and reach for their dreams of
homeownership. She has helped numerous people one on one to believe that they can have more, and this book is a manual that encompasses all the things she has learned throughout her years as a real estate agent.The book is real and relatable. She uses her own story of struggle to show others in the same situation that they too can achieve their dreams of owning their home,
I have known the writer of this book, Patricia Golden, for many years to be a person that also helps people see beyond only being able to rent and reach for their dreams of homeownership. She has helped numerous people one on one to believe that they can have more, and this book is a manual that encompasses all the things she has learned throughout her years as a real estate agent.The book is real and relatable. She uses her own story of struggle to show others in the same
situation that they too can achieve their dreams of owning their home, no matter where they started.

She is not only a real estate agent but is moving with purpose to help people "possess the land" as God commanded. The book is a great resource and allows readers to ask themselves questions that assess their readiness, in mind and in finances and then provides a systematic process to home ownership. For renters this is a great way to see if you are ready for the next step.For those that are desiring home ownership this is a great manual for guidance during the process.

The writer presents a clear overview of the obstacles that renters face, even within their own mind and maps out the ways that a renter can easily become a homeowner. The writer of this book is someone I have known for years who desires to help others achieve their dreams and with this book she does just that. The book provides a realistic process in how to go from renting to investing into a home you own. I have known Patricia Golden to be a person that believes in helping people escape the mindset of settling and empowering them to put their hands on their dream house. This book offers the same personal help she offers to her clients in a concise manual that educates and is therefore a must read for anyone interested in homeownership.

FOREWORD BY DANIEL LAVAN

Homeownership is one of the greatest joys of human life and in this book the possibilities of homeownership come to light delivering hope to individuals as well as families the great American Dream of Homeownership. This book not only gives hope but causes anyone that reads to see clearly the path to the joy of homeownership. The very thorough and detailed understanding of the process will help anyone understand and put a plan in place to reach the goal of homeownership. This book is laid out in layman's terms using easy to understand terms with a step-by-step process that is very user friendly. All basic aspects of homeownership are captured in detail in this wonderful book that is truly a road map to the AmericanDream. Patricia Golden the author, is on point in taking the fear out of the home buying process. She reaches into the heart of the homeownership process with a simplistic but manageable time frame to achieve measurable goals. Taking the fear out of the process and delivering a pathway that is both exciting and manageable. Teaching that anyone that can afford to pay a large amount for rent can definitely afford to purchase a home. She shows in the book clearly that people even with credit score issues can also have a plan that ends with homeownership. A wealth of knowledge from the beginning of the process receive the keys and walk through the doors, this book is priceless for first time homebuyers and it will assist greatly in reaching the American Dream of homeownership. until you receive the keys and walk through the doors, this book is priceless for first time homebuyers and it will assist greatly in reaching the American Dream of homeownership.

INTRODUCTION

I was born the second of seven children, but everyone thought that I was the oldest child. My mother worked two to three jobs to make ends meet for her family. While she was working, I was nurturing my siblings. I cooked, I cleaned the house, I combed my sister's hair, I washed clothes etc. to help my mother. My father did not live with us but I saw him every weekend, to collect the $15 dollars he gave my mother for the family. At the time, my father could do no wrong. He was a hard working man that worked two to three jobs also.

My father was an alcoholic who did what he knew to be a father and a husband. We lived in a two bedroom house and I promised myself that I will not live like we were living. I wanted to buy a bigger house for my mother. At the time, I did not know how that was going to happen. While listening to adults around me that had money, I noticed that most of the money came through owning their own small businesses. All the listening and learning about finances, I knew that I did not want to work all of my life. I wanted to retire, travel the world, and be able to take care of myself.

I started my love of Real Estate in 1985. I gave my life to the Lord in 1980 while in the US Army stationed in Germany. I got out of the United States Army in April 1985 after serving for 8 years and started working for the United States Postal Service in June 1985. I received a word from the Lord about Real Estate while delivering mail. I did not understand it and the more I learned the more I loved it. I delivered mail to a house that was purchased at a very

I delivered mail to a house that was purchased at a very low price and sold back with a profit made of $50,000 dollars. The contractor purchased the house and did all the renovation work. He gaveme an invitation to an event. I went to the event and learned how to buy and sell houses with other people's money. As I did the renovation on the houses, I noticed that most of the buyers coming to purchase my homes had no idea of the process. I began to develop a love for working and educating buyers. In December 1996, I got my Real Estate license. I realized that my purpose was to educate people on how to become a homeowner (how to possess the land through home ownership). I have been traveling all over educating people on the process and I know that this book will reach more people than I can in this lifetime.

CHAPTER 1 ARE YOU TIRED OF RENTING?

I ask the question because YOU really need to be tired of renting first. Take out your calculator and follow this guide and look at the results. Put the amount of your rent and how many years you have been renting into the calculator. If this does not make you tired, please call me personally. Below is an example of the average rent a person would pay:

$1000 (rent) x 12 months = $12,000 paid in a year

$12,000 x five years = $60,000 paid in five years

$12,000 x 10 years = $120,000 paid in10 years

$12,000 x 20 years = $240,000 paid in 20 years

I wanted you to see how much money has been spent and how much money has been in your hands over the many many years. This is money that could have been invested in you and your family. This was vacation money, hospital insurance, a new car, a credit card paid off, children's college paid for, down payment on another house, or just an inheritance for you to leave to your children. Instead, this money paid for another family's debts, vacations,someone else's childrens college, insurance, car payment, anotherinvestment property, etc.The only thingthat you have to show for the money that you spent is rent receipts.

You will not ever get this money back again. You can only start from this moment on to be tired of renting. Not only should you be tired of renting, but you should be tired of living with someone else and not having your own home. We all have been in this position and made this same mistake because we were not taught about investing in ourselves. Most of us did what we saw the people around us doing, which was renting or living in Public Housing.

Now that we are learning things about money and purchasing a home, we should start having this conversation with our teenagers. Now that your teenagers are learning about finances in school, I would advise giving your teenagers this book to read. Ensure that your children take all the financial classes that they can. Instead of teaching how to work for money, start teaching them how money works.

CHAPTER 2. NUMBER ONE REASON BUYERS DO NOT BUY?

There is a question that I ask when I do the home buyers seminar. My question is: What is the number one reason that people do not buy? I believe that the number one reason that people do not buy is fear. The fear of uncertainty and not knowing is common in home buying. In my 15 years of Real Estate experience, I feel that fear is number one because fear will paralyze you. Imagine this, When you are paralyzed, you are incapable of moving and going where you want to go. I have seen fear interfere with thinking, moving, breathing, feelings, and with following instructions. Fear will cause you to murmur and complain and not follow instructions. Fear will cause you not to follow up with your Realtor. The more you put it off the worse fear will affect you.The only way to conquer fear is to face it and press through to your goal.What we must learn to do is take that same fear and redirect it. Redirect it into taking action. Let the fear fuel your determination to become a homeowner.

Other reasons that people use not buy a house:
No money down
Credit no good
People are afraid of losing the house.
If I buy and need repairs how will I get the house fixed?
How will I keep up with insurance?
I am not ready, I will buy next year.
They think they cannot afford it.
Do not want the maintenance and upkeep.
Separated from spouse.
Each of these reasons is motivated and fueled by fear.
The only way to get rid of fear is to face it. Once you do that then it has no more power.

CHAPTER 3. WHAT DO I NEED TO START ?

What do you need before you can start this process is another question that I ask and is always answered wrong. Once you have overcome the fear, you must have a made up mind. In other words, you need a committed mind. A committed mind that says it does not matter what obstacles will come your way, the obstacles will not change your mind about purchasing a home. Whether there is no money down, no credit,Patricia Golden was introduced to me through my mother and we were given the opportunity to experience our home buying process with ease. I would recommend her to anyone. She is a no nonsense Realtor. Robert Hickman IRS, bad relationship, no job, no knowledge, etc, nothing will change your mind about going through this home buying process.

THERE IS A SOLUTION TO YOUR PROBLEM!!!!

This mindset I call stinking thinking. In order to overcome this mindset is to get a new mindset. Renew your mind by reading this book, being around positive people that are not jealous of you, look and see what God says about home ownership, and go back to Chapters one and Chapter two and review them again. When you start your process, do not forget to follow up and let your Realtor know your every move. Once you make the commitment, to your family, to yourself, to your Realtor, and most of all to the Process, you can become a very proud Homeowner.
NOW GO AND POSSESS THE LAND.

CHAPTER 4 WHAT IS THE PROCESS?

Once you recognize that you are tired of renting, you have no more fear, you have made up your mind, and willing to make a commitment to go through the process, there are steps that must be taken. In order to get to your destination, you must first know where you are. I hear most people say, I will buy later. My advice to them is to let us talk about your current situation. Then you will be aware of what you will need for later when your mind is ready to buy. You would have saved money, paid your bills on time, stopped paying your bills with cash, been stable on a job, etc.Start out by seeking a good mortgage company that will walk you through the financial part of home buying. If you have not owned a home in the last three years, you are considered a FIRST TIME HOME BUYER. You will be eligible for down payment and some cases closing cost assistance. If you chose to go through the first time home buyers program and get free down payment money, you must choose a mortgage company that has the money or is registered to receive it. You cannot go through any Lender because they may not have the down payment money or be qualified to receive it for their buyers. If you get approved with a mortgage company that does not have first time home buyers money, you will need to bring that down payment money to the closing table yourself. You must be able to show that you have it in the bank or that it will be gifted by someone.

You will then fill out a loan application. After that, the loan officer will give you a form to sign that will authorize them to pull your credit. Once the application and credit is looked at, the loan officer will give you a pre approval letter which states how much house you are able to purchase.

Once you sign the loan application, within three days you should receive a Good Faith Estimate. This Good Faith Estimate will give you a general idea of how much money you will need to bring to the closing table. After the loan officer has pulled your credit and looked at the loan application, He will then give you a pre approval letter. Now you must take that letter to a Realtor recommended by your Loan officer, a friend, or someone that you selected. Just insure that the Realtor has your best interest first. Do not choose a Realtor that is making all the decisions for you. You and your family will be living in the house, therefore you should pick the house. Go out with the Realtor and make a selection on a house. Make selection based on right size, number of rooms, location, etc. Do not make a selection on a house based on cosmetics that you can fix. For example, color of paint, stove and refrigerator wrong brand, or flooring etc, These are things that you can change out immediately once you purchase the house. You must understand that when you choose a house, the Realtor has to find out the proper showing instructions for getting into the house. Once you start looking at the houses, make a decision on one and let the Realtor know.

The Realtor will put an offer in for the house at the discussed price and if it is accepted then you will have a three day time period to take the earnest money deposit to only the title company chosen by the Seller. Make sure that everything that is decided on pertaining to the house is added to the contract.

So the Seller has accepted the offer. Now you must choose a professional home inspector to inspect your house and do a termite inspection. You must pay for this at the time of inspection. It is my professional opinion to be there at the time of inspection or have someone there who would understand the language of the home inspector. Someone that knows how to do handyman work, would understand the language of the home inspector when he starts describing items, and knows how to repair items in the house also. Once an inspection report is given to you, discuss the report with the Realtor. You have a time period on the contract to make a decision whether you want to proceed with the purchase of this house.You and the Realtor will discuss the report and if there are questions for the Seller, the Realtor will discuss with the Seller's Realtor. Also insure that the inspector is qualified to do a termite inspection. I recommend that you have a termite inspection. In some instances it is mandatory and in some cases not required. If there is a pool at the house, insure that the pool pump gets inspected also. It is also recommended that you have the inspector to do a wind imitigation inspection on the roof.

Sometimes your insurance company may ask for a four point inspection. If so, you can go back to the home inspector and they will complete one at an additional cost. You do not ever want to give the Lender your home inspection. The four point inspection will only include the report on the AC unit, roof, electrical. And plumbing work. Ok the inspection is completed and you would like to continue, the Lender is the only one that can order an appraisal. This appraisal will describe the property and tell the Lender the market value of the
house and houses in that area.

When the appraisal is complete, All of the paperwork will be put into an order that is required by the underwriter. The underwriter is the person that will review all paperwork for the Lender and determine whether the property and you meet the required qualifications. If you get a clear to close, This means that you have an approved loan. Before the property closes, the Lender will order a final credit report. From the time your credit was pulled by the Lender the first time until the last day, if there is any extra or new activity on your credit report it could hinder the closing. For example, inquiries, missed payments, buying something new, applying for a credit score, or paying something off could drop your credit score. The Realtor and Home Buyer will do a final walk-through inspection of the home and the Seller's Realtor will make arrangements with the Buyer's Realtor to get the keys to the house, once the closing is completed.

CHAPTER 5. WHY DO I NEED CREDIT?

You need credit because credit allows lenders access to your credit report to see how you pay your bills, so that consumers will have access to a line of credit, should they need to use it.

When Lenders look at your credit report, it gives them an idea of who you are. They are looking to see if you pay your bills on time, if you will save your money, how long you have had the debt, and how much debt you have. They look to see what your credit score is. Based on your credit score, how much debt you have, and how much income you have coming into your home, the Lender will determine how much money to lend to you. Using the same information, your interest rate will also be determined.

The Lenders will be all over the United States and they will not get to know you accept they see you on paper. That is why it is important to pay your bills on time and to have a paper trail. You cannot pay cash for everything and expect to have a paper trail. Anyone can go to the store and buy a receipt book and write up receipts.

When you pay your bills, do not use cash. If the creditor will not accept a check, then get a money order or cashiers check and make it out to who you are paying. Then make a copy After you do that, take a picture for your records. If you use your bank card, the payment will appear on your bank statement.

NEVER PAY IN CASH!!!!!!!!

CHAPTER 6. WHAT IS A CREDIT REPORT?

A credit report is a statement that has information about your credit activity and current credit situation such as loan paying history and the status of your credit accounts. Lenders use these reports to help them decide if they will loan you money and what interest rates they will offer you. Lenders also use your credit report to determine whether you continue to meet the terms of an existing credit account. Other businesses might use your credit reports to determine whether to offer you insurance, rent you a house or apartment, provide you with cable TV, internet, utilities, or cell phone service. If you agree to let an employer look at your credit report, It may also be used to make employment decisions about you. Credit reports often contain the following information Your name and any name you may have used in the past in connection with a credit account including nicknames: Current and former addresses, Birthdate, Social Security number, Phone Number Credit Accounts Current and historical, credit accounts, including the type of account (mortgage, installments, revolving, etc.) The credit limit or amount, Account balance, Account payment history, The date the account was opened and closed. The name of the creditor Collection Items, Public records, Liens Foreclosures, Bankruptcies, Civil suits and Judgements, A credit report may include information on overdue child support provided by a state or local child support agency or verified by any local, state, or government agency, INQUIRIES Companies that have accessed your credit report

CHAPTER 7. WHAT IS A CREDIT SCORE?

A credit score is a three digit number designed to represent the likelihood you pay your bills on time. The score is typically between 300-850 points designed to represent your credit risk. There are many different credit scores and scoring models. Higher credit scores generally result in more favorable credit terms. Credit scores are calculated using information in your credit reports including your payment history, the amount of debt you have, and the length of your credit history. Higher scores mean you have demonstrated responsible credit behavior in the past, which may make potential lenders and creditors more confident when evaluating a request for credit.

Here is a general look at credit score ranges:

300-579 Poor

580-669 Fair

670-739 Good

740-799 Very Good

800-850 Excellent

There are dozens of credit reporting agencies, however, there are three national credit bureaus, (Equifax,Transunion, and Experian) that compete to capture, update, and store credit history on all consumers. Each Creditor decides who they will report to 1, 2, or all 3 bureaus.

CHAPTER 8. WHAT KIND OF LOAN CAN I GET?

A lot of potential homebuyers tell me that they are going to start buying next year. I tell them that in order to buy next year, you must Know where you are so that you will know where you are going. In other words you need to see a lender and let them tell you what is required to get a loan approved. When you finally decide to go and see the lender, usually there are things that you could have been working on the entire year while you were waiting.

For example a lot of people pay their rent with cash and get a receipt. No No No No. Ask your landlord can you pay by check, money order, bank draft, or other means besides cash. You must have a reliable money trail and it must be well documented.

There are several businesses where payments are made in cash only. People have jobs doing hair and lawn servicing to make a living. Whatever you do to earn an income and money is paid to you in cash, put that money in a reliable, traceable bank account. If you need to take the money out to pay bills, deposit the money first. If you take the money out, make sure you keep receipts for what you spend that money on.

The Lender will advise you on the different types of loans that are available. I would like to go over a few choices.

FHA insured Loan is a Federal Housing Administration mortgage which is provided by an FHA approved lender. They are popular among first time home buyers because they allow down payment of 3.5% for credit scores of 580 and above.

However, borrowers must pay mortgage insurance premiums (PMI), which protects the lender if a borrower (defaults). if this loan goes into default, the Federal Housing Administration pays the Lender the balance on the loan and takes possession of the property and it becomes a HUD Property. These properties will go back on the (market), but the properties will go through a bidding process. All properties will be sold in the condition that they are in. FHA loans come in fixed-rate terms of 15 and 30 years.

Veterans Administration (VA) loan is a mortgage loan that is issued by private lenders and backed by and guaranteed by the United States Department of Veterans Affairs(VA). The intention of the program is to supply home financing to eligible veterans to purchase properties.

The next type of loan is a Conventional Loan that is not GUARANTEED or INSURED by any government agency, including the Federal Housing Administration (FHA), the Farmers Home Administration (FmHA), and the Department of Veterans Affairs (VA).

Here is a list of common paperwork that most Lenders
are going to ask you for:

Pay check stubs(For part time job also)
2 to 3 years Income Taxes with w-2s (If self-employed
need profit and loss statements also)
Reward Letter (Proof of Social Security)
Proof of Marriage and Divorce
Gift letters (If using gift funds)
Photo ID
2 to 3 Years of Bank Statements and any other assets
Any other Income Verification

Alimony or Child Support
(your choice if you choose to use)

Retirement and Investment Accounts
Proof of Retirement Income (If retired)
Bankruptcy or Foreclosure Paperwork (If needed)
Verification of Rent (Lender will request)
Verification of Employment (Lender will request)
Proof of Permanent Residence

CHAPTER 9. WHAT ARE CLOSING COSTS?

Closing costs are fees paid for the services and expenses required to finalize a mortgage at the closing of a real estate transaction.Closing costs are incurred by the Buyer and the Seller. As a rule of thumb, closing cost is usually 2 - 4% of the purchase price. The lender is required to outline your closing costs in the Loan Estimate you receive when you first apply for the loan and in the Closing Disclosure documents you receive in the days before the closing.

Here is a list of some closing costs.
BUYERS
Escrow deposit
Real Estate Fees
Seller Concessions
Processing Fee
Loan origination fee
Municipal lien search
Underwriting fee
Title search fee
Prepaid interest
Flood certification
Recording fee (deed)
Recording fee (mortgage)
HOA Dues
Property Taxes
Lenders title insurance
survey

CHAPTER 10. WHAT IS DOWN PAYMENT?

Down payment is the part of the loan that the lender is asking you to bring to the table.

For example: If the lender approves you for a $100,000 loan and the lender will only bring $95,000(95%) of the loan to the closing table, you are then required to bring the $5,000 (5%), the $5,000 is your down payment. If you are asked what your Loan to value(LTV), you can say 95% which is how much the lender is bringing to the closing table.

The Lender will not allow down payment money to be paid by anyone except a non profit organization approved to give the money.

This money will have guidelines that the Lender will give you. You can also get down payment money from a relative or friend that will give you a gift that does not need to be paid back. The lender will require a gift letter to be written by the person giving the gift, stating that this money does not need to be paid back at any time. In some instances, the underwriter will require proof that the gift came from the givers bank account. When you decide to purchase a home, you must begin to save money.

When you start to save money, you must save it and act as
if it is not there. When your car does not start, and when
someone needs their rent paid, and when you want to eat
out, Act as if that money does not exist. In reality it does not
exist. If you have not owned a home in the last three years,
you
would be considered a first time home buyer. There are
programs available to assist you with your down payment,
and in some cases, closing cost. This money does not need
to be paid back, but it will be satisfied in portions based on
the terms by the non profit that is bringing the money to the
table. For example, if you are given $10,000 over a 5 year
period, $2,000 will be satisfied every year for
5 years until you do not owe the $10,000.

CHAPTER 11. THE ROLE OF THE REALTORS

Purchasing a home can be a bumpy and difficult process. Sometimes there are many surprises that are unexpected. Therefore, A Buyers Agent role is to be that professional Realtor that will lead you into the Home buying process. Sometimes you will be referred to a lender that will best help you accomplish your home buyers purchase. A Professional Buyer's Agent will find out the Lenders in the area that will best serve the Buyers by being familiar with the Lenders in the area that are offering Down Payment and closing cost assistance.

Realtors should be able to advise you on knowing about the procuring cause. Which means Buyers should not talk to are go see houses without your agent being with you. Real Estate agents work by a code of ethics. When there is a problem with a Realtor there are places that you can go to get help. Sometimes it might entail you receiving money back, that you might have lost.

CHAPTER 12. DO'S AND DON'TS OF BUYERS

Do not give money to anyone but the title company. Do not talk to a seller or go to a new home construction site without letting them know that you have a Realtor. Usually the new home construction Realtor will allow you to sign in your Realtor and show you the property. Your Realtor must be the procuring cause (reason) of you finding the property.

Do not purchase a home without having a home inspection.

-Do not pay your bills with cash

-Do not go looking for houses and you have not been approved.

-Do not let your emotions get the best of you.

-Do not make any large or small purchases before you purchase your home.

-Do not quit or switch jobs

-Do not be late on your bills.

-Do not negotiate or discuss the sale price or closing cost on any property that is for the Realtor to do.

-Do not trust everything you read in ads

-Do not sign a contract without both husband and wife approval of the house.

-Do not close or open any credit cards.

-Do not make payments on collection accounts.

CHAPTER 13. YOU ARE CLEAR TO CLOSE

Clear to Close is what everyone involved in this process wants to hear. A clear to close means that the loan 70 has been approved. Once the processor gathers all your paperwork together, puts the paperwork in the order requested, and submit it to the underwriter, a decision will be made. When the approval comes from the underwriter, this is called a clear to close. The Title Company will go over the contract to make sure there are no seller concessions. No other invoices that need to be paid, or other monies to be paid by the buyer.

The Title Company will instruct you to get your home warranty company to send an invoice over if a home warranty is being purchased.
The Title Company will do the prorations on the property taxes, insurance, and any other finances that need to be prorated
The Title Company will instruct you on all identification that you must bring with you to the closing table.
The Title Company will also let you know whether you need to bring any money to the closing table.
The Title Company will issue Title Insurance Policies for the protection of the homeowner and the mortgage lender
The Title Company notarizes all documents at closing.
The Title Company Records all documents after closing.
The Title Company collects all monies due and distributes them to the proper parties; including satisfying any outstanding mortgages; judgement and liens.

The Title Company maintains escrow funds with a FDIC Lender.

The Title Company will provide you with information on Homestead Exemption

On the day of closing, you will have a final walk thru inspection. The Title company will inform you where the location of the closing will take place.

When you arrive, you will sign all paperwork that is required by everyone involved in this process.

After all monies are collected,
the title company will send all paperwork to
the bank to accept. Once the bank has accepted the paperwork then you will be a Homeowner.

The title company will send the signed deed to the county or city administration office to record and you will then be sent a copy of the recorded deed. You are to take this recorded deed to file homestead exemption on your property.

Once you have talked to your Realtor or Lender and have been given instructions, please follow up with them and let them know what you have decided to do. My license allows me to work in the state of Florida. I am also a part of a National Organization of Realtors that qualifies me to work in all states.

*Do not hesitate to contact me anytime through my email or website 1RealEstateProblemSolver@gmail.com.

CONGRATULATIONS FOR GOING THRU
THE PROCESS!!!!!!

Testimonials

Patricia Golden assisted us in purchasing our first home in 2013. She assisted us step by step and introduced us to many benefits from being a first time home buyer. We would recommend her to anyone that is searching.

Calvin and Kimberly Lawrence

I was assisting my husband's aunt in selling her home. Her being 85 years old would have been difficult for her to move. So Patricia Golden advertised the house for a Seller that would rent the house back to my aunt.

Vivian Scott Chew

I moved from New York to Florida and Patricia Golden assisted me in the purchase of my home. I had several Realtors trying to tell me what to buy instead of allowing me to decide. Patricia allowed me to make my own choice without any pressure.

Princess Worrell

My family and I were searching for our first home and Paticia Golden stepped in and guided us through the process. She assisted us in getting down payment and closing cost assistant. When we wanted to give up, she encouraged us to continue because we would see our house and know it.

Angeline and Timothy Rhodes

Patricia Golden was introduced to me through my mother and we were given the opportunity to experience our home buying process with ease. I would recommend her to anyone. She is a no nonsense Realtor.

Robert Hickman

Patricia Golden

My name is Patricia Golden and I am 62 years young. I was born in Winter Park, Fl and raised in Eatonville, Fl. When the schools were segregated, I was going to the 7th grade. By that time I was already cooking and taking care of my sisters and brothers. I became pregnant at the age of 15 years old.. While in school, I veered toward business classes and junior achievement. I went to night classes to make up for classes I missed while having my son. Going to night classes, I experienced some life changing events. I succeeded in graduating with my class of1974 and the next day I was hired at (Orange Memorial Hospital) now known as Orlando Regional Hospital as an Emergency Room Secretary. I worked there until I left to join the USArmy in April 1977.

I served for 8 years as a Legal Clerk court Reporter for my Battalions. My second tour of Germany in 1982, I received Jesus Christ as my Lord and Savior. I left the military in April 1985 and started working for the US Postal Service as a Letter Carrier. I retired in 1996 and went to school to receive my Real Estate License. Not really understanding what my purpose was, I kept seeking the Lord until I got a clear direction on what He wanted me to do.. During my seeking the Lord, He gave me a passion to help His people Possess The Land Through Homeownership. I began buying and fixing up houses to sell. While doing this, I came in contact with a lot of Buyers that wanted to purchase my home, but knew nothing about the Home buying process. Also, I met several people that wanted to rent my home and had no desire to be a homeowner for several reasons that I mention in the book Possessing The Land Through Homeownership. Since then, I have been educating God's people on the process of home ownership. Also what the Lord says concerning home ownership. This book will educate, inspire, and guide you into the purchase of your first home.

www.ingramcontent.com/pod-product-compliance
Lightning Source LLC
Chambersburg PA
CBHW061447050726
47593CB00004B/1497